HOUSE

of the

GUARDIAN ANGEL

Gemini Krikkett

AuthorHouse™
1663 Liberty Drive
Bloomington, IN 47403
www.authorhouse.com
Phone: 833-262-8899

Because of the dynamic nature of the Internet, any web addresses or links contained in this book may have changed since publication and may no longer be valid. The views expressed in this work are solely those of the author and do not necessarily reflect the views of the publisher, and the publisher hereby disclaims any responsibility for them.

This book is printed on acid-free paper.

ISBN: 978-1-6655-6669-8 (sc)
ISBN: 978-1-6655-6671-1 (hc)
ISBN: 978-1-6655-6670-4 (e)

Library of Congress Control Number: 2022913953

Print information available on the last page.

Published by AuthorHouse 08/26/2022

authorHOUSE®

Dedicated to my most unlikely of friends.
You know who you are, and my world
would not be the same without you!

I was walking on the beach near where I live in San Diego when I looked down and there on the sand lay a perfect and whole sand dollar.

For those who have searched for the perfectly elusive sand dollar, unbroken by the sea or time, it is a rare occurrence that may take hours or days to achieve. I have friends who have never had such a blessing occur.

I pulled a napkin from my pocket and I very gingerly picked it up. I wrapped the shell carefully before putting it into the pocket of my sweater where I hoped it would be safe until I got home.

Finishing the walk on the beach I thought back to the first time I had ever seen such a sand dollar. I find it hard to believe that this happened almost a half of a century ago. I couldn't have been more than a handful in years and we were visiting my mother's grandmother. That day is one of the only memories that I have of her. I am sure that it is because of the sand dollar she had on the mantle of the fireplace that I remember this day at all.

You see, while my mother and she had tea and visited, I had already seen the special shell. It was beautiful and perfect and white -and it was just out of my reach!

Grandma's House

My mother says that I was always a curtain climber, and I guess that this day proved it. I began with a folding chair and added a small stool to the seat of the chair. I even thought to place a fluffy pillow over the stool, just in case, before I strategically began to climb my creative version of a ladder. I was still just a little out of reach. I got on my tip toes, wiggling my fingers and hoping to somehow grow the extra two inches necessary to be able to claim my prize when I was snatched quickly from behind.

Suddenly my mother was yelling at me and it looked like her granny was trying not to cry. In her hands she protectively held the sand dollar that I had tried so hard to reach. Her breathing was labored and there was a sad shine in her eyes that threatened to spill over onto her weathered and lined cheeks.

I didn't understand. I had just wanted to see the pretty shell. I began to cry tearfully the way small children will when denied their heart's desire, until Granny asked me in a cracked and ancient voice,

"Have I ever told you how God gave the sand dollars to the Guardian Angels to live in?"

My tears were forgotten as I shook my head and wondered how the angels would fit inside, and would there be enough room to move about? What about their wings? They must be smaller than Tinkerbell, who I had seen on Disney's Peter Pan and fallen in love with.

"You see this shell was given to me many years ago by a pastor who saw me grieving after the death of my son, your great-uncle Johnny. You see, out of all my children he was the one that I worried about. In high school Johnny had a sweetheart, and he loved her and thought she loved him. After graduation she said that it was over and she moved away to college. Johnny was never the same. He took up motorcycles and ran with a rough crowd. Soon he found himself in front of a Judge who gave him the choice of going to prison or going into the military to fight the Vietnamese war."

She shook her head sadly and took a deep breath before continuing.

"So my lost boy went off to fight in a war that he didn't even believe in, and he died there. I worried that his soul would never rest right, and my pastor saw how inconsolable I was. So one Sunday after services he gave me this sand dollar and then he told me the story of how God gave the sand dollars to the Guardian Angels to live in." She paused to let that sink in.

"That's right. It all started a long time ago, just about at the dawn of time I would say. Certainly the dawn of humanity. Do you know the story of Adam and Eve?"

She saw that even if I had heard the names, the details were lost to my young mind. She filled in the important stuff.

'Adam was the first man made by God, and Eve was made to be his mate. God gave his Garden of Eden to them to live in. They could do whatever they wanted to, with one exception. The largest tree in the center of the garden was off limits. Called the Tree of Knowledge, it was the only thing they were forbidden. But God also gave the two of them the freedom to choose for themselves, to make their own decisions. That was something that he hadn't even given his Angels- and they had been been around for eons before Adam and Eve showed up. Because of this the Angels didn't really like the humans much, but they tolerated them and left them alone like God had instructed.

So when the day came that Eve was tricked by the Devil into eating one of the precious fruits from the Tree of Knowledge the angels had very little sympathy for the humans. They all whispered among themselves, saying that they knew that it would come to no good with those pesky humans. It was just a matter of time. They watched as Adam and Eve were evicted from The Garden of Eden and forbidden from returning for their disobedience."

She paused for a moment and stared right at me and shook a finger as she said, "You remember that when you want to disobey your mother!"

"Now the very first night for Adam and Eve was nothing nice. Imagine that they had never been hungry before, or cold, or tired. They tried everything they could conceive of to try to get back into Eden. They apologized, begged, cried, they made promises that they would never again disobey the One Rule. But they had eaten from the Tree of Knowledge, and that couldn't be undone.

Eventually God got tired of them trying to sneak back into the Garden Of Eden and he placed an Angel at the gate to keep them from getting back in. He gave the angel a flaming sword to use if he found it was needed, and was told that he should encourage the pair of disobedient humans to leave the proximity by any means necessary.

So the angel watched the painful birth of humanity, with all the loud cries and tearful pleas that turned into a panic that even the animals couldn't ignore when the sun went down that first night! Can you imagine? They didn't know if it was ever coming back, that they had been cast into darkness as part of their punishment!

Fear was our first natural instinct, and that is still true today. They were afraid of everything, and their pitiful cries kept even the most fierce of the animals at bay that first night. Needless to say that no one got any sleep!

And all the while the Angel watched.

Eventually the angel went to God and asked about the fate and future of the humans.

"I know that you are mad at the kids for their disobedience, I get it. But aren't you going to do something? Look at how pitiful they are!"

God considered the request and came up with a solution to the problem.

"You want me to help? I will tell you what, why don't YOU help? Anyone who wants to help you help the humans has my blessing. I will even give you a gift that has everything you need for your most noble quest."

He reached into his robe and with a flourish pulled out a small flat disk.

"You see this, it has a hole in the back of it. If you go in through the hole then you will come out through the falling star in the front. That is the roadmap back to Heaven, so that nobody gets lost."

He turned the sand dollar over to show the design on the front.

"Here is the design of a leaf, for growth and for nourishment. If you step back from the leaf then you will see the semblance of a campfire. That is for light and for warmth."

God took the disk and began to work it between his hands as he continued.

"Everything you need to help the humans is right here, but you have to hold up your end of the bargain. If you ever come across any lost souls, souls that are hurt, needing to rest and find a better way then you must invite them in to rest and heal, and then SHOW them a better way."

As he finished speaking he began to rain the sand dollars from heaven to the earth. One disk became a thousand and then maybe a million as they found their way to the shores of the land below.

"To make sure that those troublesome humans don't interfere with you and your crew and yet you are still close enough to help them, I will put these in the shores and shallows of the worlds oceans. I don't want the humans to ever try to decide where the important blessings go."

And then God nodded to the Angel, his signal of dismissal, and turned away to other important things.

Granny looked very serious as she wound her story to a close.

"That clause in the deal that God made with the Angels had one other side effect that can be taken as proof that the Guardian Angels inhabit these perfect little shells. If you ever break one open that you find whole on the beach, then you will find up to five perfect white Doves of Peace, in full flight form with wings that have feathers so fine that you can practically count them individually, even though they are smaller than your pinky nail! It is said that those Doves of Peace represent one for every soul that has been saved through that particular shell."

I begged her to show me the doves but she refused, saying that I would have to find my own one day to see if the story was true.

As I returned home from my walk I carefully reached into my pocket to retrieve my sand dollar. I was at first disappointed that I didn't find the whole shell that I had started with. Then I realized that In its place were two halves, a falling star and five beautiful white doves of peace. And you know what? She was right, I could count the feathers on the wings!

So if you have a Guardian Angel who needs a house, or a lost soul who needs a place to rest then maybe you should go to the beach and try to find your very own 'House of the Guardian Angel'. They will love it!

If you would like more information on ordering your very own "House of the Guardian Angel", (which is an individually designed Energy Item Sand Dollar), created by the artist and author, Gemini Krikkett, please contact via email at krikkettg@gmail.com to request a current inventory list.

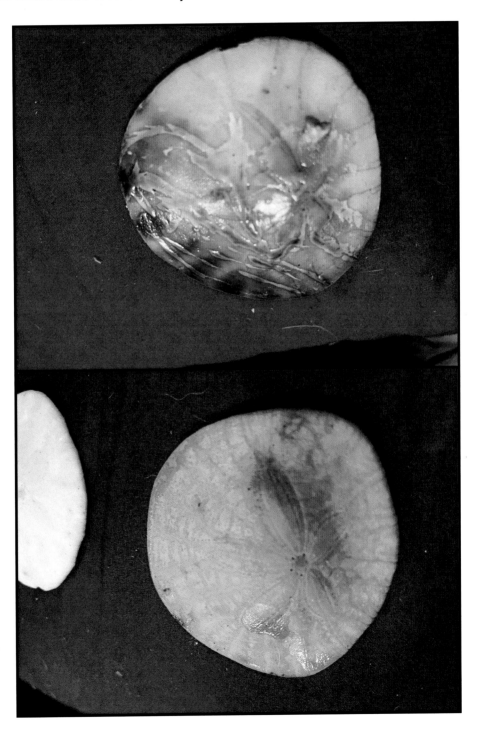

Printed in the United States
by Baker & Taylor Publisher Services